TRACY AUSTIN

by Gloria D. Miklowitz

tempo
books

GROSSET & DUNLAP
A FILMWAYS COMPANY
Publishers • New York

Acknowledgements:

Special thanks for the help given me to Mr. and Mrs. Bob Henry, Dr. and Mrs. Donald Corbett and Coaches Robert Lansdorp and Vic Braden.

PICTURE CREDITS:

Vic Braden, pages viii, 7, 11, 23, 31; Kelly Henry, pages 38, 39; Los Angeles Times, page 53; Dr. Dave Powell, page 16; John Zimmerman for Sports Illustrated © 1978 Time, Inc., page 5; Tony Korody-Sygma, pages 28, 86; Wide World, pages vii, 35, 41, 48, 52, 57, 60, 65, 68, 71, 72, 75, 77, 79, 80, 82, 83, 85; World Tennis magazine, page 3.

CONTENTS

The joy victory brings. Tracy scores a match point at the U.S. Open Tennis Championships and beats Heidi Eisterlehner of West Germany.

Tracy as a youngster off to a winning start.

CHAPTER ONE

TENNIS FROM THE CRADLE

There's a story going around about Tracy Austin, the 14-year-old super kid of tennis. Youngest to play at Wimbledon in its hundred year history, they say she cut her teeth on a tennis ball instead of a teething ring. It may be a tall tale, but there's more than a little truth to it.

Vic Braden, well-known tennis Pro, says he was rolling a ball inside Tracy's carriage when she was eight months old. At two, he was throwing balls to her. At three, he was giving her lessons.

George Austin, Tracy's father, says that, at two, Tracy was breaking everything in the living room. So, older brother Doug bought her a present. A tennis-size ball made of yarn to throw around or tear apart.

Certainly, tennis has been part of Tracy's life from her first days. As an infant, she slept in the back of the family station wagon while mom and dad played on the nearby courts. As a toddler, she peered through the bars of her playpen. Her parents were doing funny things: smashing balls across a net, spinning serves, lobbing, rallying fiercely. Music, for most children her age, was "I'm a Little Teapot." For Tracy, music was the sound of tennis balls hitting smack in the center of a racket.

Back when she wasn't yet a tennis wonder kid, *World Tennis* Magazine

world/tennis

Tracy, at four, on the cover of World Tennis *magazine.*

pictured her on its cover. She was only four, but the editor loved the shot of a funny-looking kid in blue sneakers holding a tennis racket.

Born December 12, 1962, Tracy was 15 in 1977. Only a few months before her birthday, she had startled the tennis world. She beat the world's fourth-ranked woman player, Sue Barker, at Forest Hills. By the end of that great summer, Tracy was the Nadia Comaneci of the tennis world. She ranked top nationally in the 14-and-under class and top in the 16-and-under. And, she reached the quarter-finals at Forest Hills.

Swinging a tennis racket at age three is no guarantee of tennis stardom. But it helps. So does having a family devoted to the game. And Tracy's family—mother; father; Pam, 27; Jeff, 25; Doug, 23; John, 20—are all into the

The Austin family and their trophies. Standing left to right: Jeff, Doug, Pam, John. Sitting: George, Tracy, Jeanne.

sport. In 1976 they were photographed standing before their tennis trophies, about 400 of them. There were nine national championships among them. A year later the shelves bulged with quite a few more. 130 of those statues, plates and silver bowls were inscribed with Tracy's name.

The Austin family lives in Rolling Hills Estates, California, a city near Los Angeles. Tracy's dad, George, works as a nuclear physicist for an aerospace company. He met Jeanne, Tracy's mother, while they were both students in college. After they married, they moved around a lot because George was in the Air Force. But by 1955, they settled in southern California.

Jeanne Austin took up tennis for exercise after John, her fourth child, was born. Her only link with tennis until then was a brother. He had played in

Tracy, age 5, says goodbye to her brother, Jeff, who is leaving for the summer junior circuit.

college and held a national ranking. Jeanne became quite good in the next years. In 1961 she ranked 25th in the southern California women's division. She began playing in mixed doubles tournaments with George. Then, in 1962 Tracy was born.

While George and Jeanne Austin played tennis, the older children played nearby. They built sand forts while Tracy slept in the station wagon.

When Tracy was two, Vic Braden built and became the director and Pro at the new Jack Kramer Tennis Club in Rolling Hills Estates. Jeanne wanted to give the children a good start in the game she and her husband loved. So, she took a job at the tennis shop to help pay for lessons.

"My husband and I got interested in it [tennis] and when we started, the children—Pam and Jeff—loved it," Mrs.

Austin says. "The other kids came along
... when they saw everyone doing
it." It's been good for the children, the
Austins believe. They've gained poise,
and have traveled and seen a lot.

The first child to take lessons was
Pam. She wasn't like Tracy. Tracy entered tournaments at seven and won her
first at nine. Pam was a late starter. She
didn't begin competitive play till she
was 11, two years before Tracy was
born. At first, she didn't like the game.
Her mother paid her 25¢ an hour to play.

"She pushed me and I really re-
sented it at first. But she made me play
to the point where I was good enough to
like it," Pam says.

Pam was 14 or so before she began
winning. By 16 she was a member of the
U.S. Junior Wightman Cup team, and
national hard court doubles champ
(1968). But it wasn't until after her first

year at college that she really got hooked. Then, a South African urged her to try the tennis tour in his country. She quit school and flew to South Africa. After that, she could hardly get enough of tennis in foreign places. When she played at Wimbledon, she wrote home about the exciting places she saw, not about the game scores.

Pam played three years on the Virginia Slims tour and two seasons with the Phoenix Racquets of World Team Tennis. Now she works for the L.A. Strings and teaches tennis.

Jeff gave up the tennis circuit only recently. But before he did, the shrimp of the family (he's 5'10", shorter than Pam) was ranked 26th among United States Tennis Association (USTA) men in 1974. Along the way he won the southern California doubles championships in the 14, 16, and 18 age group. He won

Tracy, age 7, with mother Jeanne, sister Pam and brother John; taking Pam to the airport for the start of a tournament circuit.

the Orange Bowl doubles titles with Guillermo Vilas in 1967. For three years he played on the U.S. Junior Davis Cup Team.

An All-American at UCLA from 1971-73, he was a member of two NCAA championship teams. He won the national hardcourts title at Aptos, California after his senior year. Jeff says he was always driven by an absolute refusal to accept defeat. In 1977 he began his first year at UCLA Law School.

Doug, a Long Beach State college graduate, works in the construction business. He always played tennis "just hard enough to get by," his mother says. Still, he ranked in the top 10 in his age group in southern California. He led the Rolling Hills High School tennis team. In college, he was content to just be No. 1 in tennis at his school.

John, 20, and Tracy are the only two

Austins still competing. A junior at UCLA, John's majoring in Economics. He says he took Economics so he can learn how to manage all the money he's going to win. He'll turn pro after he graduates.

"Tennis is what I want to do more than anything," he says. But it wasn't always so. He started playing at 10 and hated it at first, like Pam. "My mom made me do it. She said I had to hit every day. I wanted to goof around with my friends, but then I got to like tennis. Now, I just love to travel and play."

When the children were small, Jeanne Austin urged them to call their friends on Sunday nights to "make tennis dates for every day of the week." They each had little date books to keep track of appointments. "Practice was routine," she says. "I just told my kids, 'Next week you'll have to play Suzie Q.

You don't want her to beat you, so you practice.'"

Her advice paid off. Every one of the Austin children took to tennis. The desire to win burned in most of them.

John, now aiming for the No. 1 spot on his college tennis team, has won a good share of titles. He took the National Indoor Doubles and played on the Junior Davis Cup team. He reached the finals of the National Boys 18-and-under. In 1976 he played on the satellite circuit in the East. He was No. 5 on the UCLA tennis team.

But of all the Austins, it's Tracy the family feels shows the most talent. Jeff says his sister's *intensity* is what makes her so great. "What's amazing is that when Tracy plays for four hours, she *thinks* for four hours." And no matter how tired she gets, she never gives up.

Pam says, "She gives no excuses for losing. I don't know where she gets that. Most everybody in our family except John tends to rationalize." Pam tells how Tracy threw up during a match and lost. Mrs. Austin tried to comfort her. "No one can expect to win while she's sick," she said. Tracy answered, "Mom. You can't have any excuses when you lose."

That's the kind of attitude that makes a winner, many think. And Tracy, at 15, is a winner on her way to a career that could outshine Chris Evert's. For the Austin family, little Tracy may be the six million dollar baby.

CHAPTER TWO

THE ROAD TO WIMBLEDON

For Tracy, that yellow brick road which led to Wimbledon began on tennis courts early. "I think my father put a racket in my hand when I was two days old," she says.

Though her first lessons were at three, she didn't enter tournaments until the ripe old age of seven! At that time the Austins registered her with the Southern California Tennis Association (SCTA), junior division. For a small fee

Tracy, age 4, working out with her first coach, Vic Braden.

she began receiving the annual schedule of tournaments sanctioned by her
section. (The United States is divided
into 17 sections. Southern California is
one.) She began competing in the 10's-
and-under, and 12's-and-under girls'
games.

Tracy practiced regularly every day
after school and on weekends. She began taking lessons from Robert Lansdorp, when Braden left the Kramer
club. At first it was a half hour a week.
As the family finances improved, she
took more lessons. Lansdorp is still Tracy's coach, and the Austins credit him
with their daughter's success.

Weekends, Tracy's parents toted
her to tournaments. Sometimes, it meant
getting up as early as five in the morning
to drive to Santa Barbara in time for
breakfast before the games. Tracy
wasn't the only one in the family in-

volved in tournaments at the time. Mrs. Austin was the family chauffeur and scheduler. She had to have the mind of a computer to keep her children's activities straight. Which Austin child needed to be picked up at school? Which was due at tennis lessons or practice? Which tournaments would be best to enter for each of the children? What were the entry date deadlines? And finally, how to be in more than one place at once when more than one child was playing a weekend tournament?

Tracy was good from the first. Seeing how hard her sister and brothers worked, and hearing about their successes made her want to win, too.

The first tournament she played was against Julie Kramer. Julie was five years older than Tracy, and won. Tracy broke down and cried.

At the age of nine, Tracy took her

first trophies. She beat Shelly Stillman of Encinitas, 6-4, 6-0 for the 12-and-under title in the L.A. Junior Tennis tourney at Griffith Park. She also won the 10-and-under division by beating Kelly Henry of Glendale 6-0, 6-4.

By 10, Tracy's long list of wins in her section qualified her for national competition among juniors. Now the mail brought a new list of tournaments for 12's, 14's and 16's. These games were played in other parts of the country. Only the very best players from each section could go to the Nationals.

In the next three years Tracy took trophies like she was collecting bottle caps.

> —The U.S. public parks' 12-and-under (for three different years).
> —the national 12-and-under singles and doubles.
> —the U.S. 12-and-under indoor sin-

gles and doubles (at age 10).

—the U.S. 14-and-under indoor singles, twice.

—the national 14-and-under singles championship.

Tracy won the first of her national indoor titles at Harry Hopman's Tennis Academy in Port Washington, N.Y. The Austins asked the old tennis master, "How should Tracy train? What could she do to improve?" Hopman replied, "What do you tell a genius?"

In 1975, when she was 12, Tracy crushed everyone she met in the national 14's at Shreveport, La. Then, she entered the 16's in Charleston, W. Va. Playing against girls as much as four years older, and a lot bigger, she reached the third round, where she was beaten 7-5 in the third set.

Tracy is so competitive that the loss really threw her. She phoned her father and cried, "I can't stand it, Dad. I'm so sick of losing!" Yet, the last time she had lost to any girl in her own age group was five years before!

The emotional strain of national competition isn't for everyone. There's the excitement of air travel. There may be time-zone differences to adjust to. Food and water changes may affect the stomach badly. There's the worry of schoolwork waiting at home to catch up with. There's the thrill of seeing new places and meeting new people. To that is added the anxiety of the tournament ahead, and the disappointment, if you lose.

One 11-year-old, staying in a strange home in a distant city, received a call from her father. He tore into her about how badly she had played that day. Upset, she roamed her hosts' home at three in the morning. When asked

Tracy, age 5, with Francoise Durr, one of the top players on the women's circuit.

what she was looking for, she said, "Something to hug."

The Austins say they never pressure Tracy. When she had the chance to play in Japan, Mrs. Austin would have liked to go there to Christmas shop. But Tracy didn't want to miss school. Her wishes were respected and the trip was turned down. "Why should I pressure her?" Mrs. Austin asks. "This game is still supposed to be fun."

The Austins try to keep life normal for Tracy. After school her mother picks her up in the family station wagon. She changes into tennis clothes in the car. "Can't waste time. Got to hit the deck, swinging the racket," she'll say as they drive to the courts. After three or four hours of practice, it's home for dinner and homework.

In junior high, Tracy's favorite class was physical education. Her interests included collecting stamps, coins, stuffed animals and stickers to put on her notebooks. She liked to read the Nancy Drew books, as well as *Charlotte's Web*. Her idea of a really special day was a trip to Disneyland.

A very good student, Tracy cares about her schoolwork. In fourth grade, her brother says, she stayed up for three nights. She was trying to finish her math homework for the whole year.

At Rolling Hills High School this year, she's in ninth grade. Her first semester program is light—English, typing, western civilization, public speaking, and office assistant. Because she's away at tournaments about one out of every five school days, she takes books and school assignments with her. Often, she does homework on planes.

"I want to be Number One," Tracy has said. A lot of people want to be best.

But to reach that goal requires sacrifices few are willing to make.

In the case of a junior tennis player, it may mean giving up a part in the school play. Those hours rehearsing are traded for hours on the tennis courts. Maybe you can improve the lob, or serve, or some other weakness.

The best example of Tracy's dedication to her sport comes from Kelly Henry, Tracy's friend and tennis competitor. "We were in New York together, the day after a big tournament. Our hosts said they'd arranged a big treat. Dinner at a fancy restaurant, and tickets to a terrific play afterwards." Tracy was the only one of the group that didn't go along. She said she had a couple hours of practice to put in yet. And then she had to go to bed early.

Despite the attention her success brings, Tracy remains a nice kid. In 1974 she was voted "most popular" by the very girls she was competing with and beating in the 12-and-under girls' nationals. That's some compliment.

But maybe Tracy's behavior comes from her mother's attitude. Victories are fine, Mrs. Austin says. But what really matters is to be polite, kind, and to behave like a young lady. "Then," she says, "you'll always be a champion."

Tracy, a conscientious student, works on her homework.

CHAPTER THREE

THE KID PLAYS THE PROS

At seven, Tracy was just starting into junior competition. Wimbledon and Forest Hills, places most children her age had never heard of, were still seven years away. These were places to dream about, to whisper of with awe and longing. Only the greats made it there.

But by the time Tracy was 11, Wimbledon seemed a bit closer. On July 28, 1974, she won the singles title of the USLTA tournament for girls 12-and-under. Top seeded player, she beat No. 2 seed Kelly Henry of Glendale, Ca., 6-4, 6-2 at Savannah, Ga.

Just before her 12th birthday in December, the L.A. Strings made a surprising announcement. They wanted to draft Tracy for World Team Tennis. It was a reward for her interest in the Strings.

The draft was a kind of joke, because others drafted included Johnny Carson and Dean Martin, Jr. Tracy couldn't play on WTT without being a pro. The general manager of the Strings had some nice things to say about Tracy. "She has much potential," he said. "If she matures at the same rate, she's going to be dynamite. She'll be one of the best players in the country."

Tournament followed tournament in the next months, and the trophy shelves became more crowded. Then, in

Tracy, age 10, competing in a celebrity event with Mickey Dolenz of the "Monkees".

1976, a cover picture of Tracy and a story on the family appeared in *Sports Illustrated* Magazine. The story brought many fan letters. But its real importance was this: It announced to the world—Watch Tracy Austin. This girl is going places!

Shortly after the article appeared, Tracy attended the first Annual Tennis Tournament of Champions. Sponsored by *Seventeen* Magazine, it was held in Merrifield, Va. Each state, except Alaska, sent their best female players in each of four age groups (14, 16, 18, and 21-and-under). From the 200 top players, four winners emerged. Guess who was one of them? Right. None other than little Tracy.

Came summer, and Tracy played a fun exhibition. This time it was against Bobby Riggs. Riggs was 58, a former

Wimbledon winner, and a real male chauvinist. He had played and lost to Billie Jean King. He had beat Tracy two years before in an exhibition game. Had Tracy improved since then?

Tracy broke Riggs' first two services for a 4-0 advantage. Then Riggs got down to business. He struggled to break her serve and pulled within 4-2. Tracy giggled as the crowd cheered her shots. She put Riggs away in two more games.

"My strategy was to just keep it steady and maybe, because he was old, he'd get tired," she said.

After the match, Tracy was handed a big bouquet of roses. Poor Bobby. He was handed an armful of weeds!

In August, Tracy defended her national championship 14-and-under title in the finals of the National Girls 14 Tennis Championships. She had not lost a set all year. She controlled the match after forcing Pam Shriver away from the net again and again. "When I could get to the net, she would hit such high lobs that I couldn't hit overhead returns," Shriver said.

On September 8th, she took two championships in the 48th Santa Monica Tennis Classic. First, she defeated Anna Maria Fernandez of Torrance to win the Open Women's Division. Then she ousted Shelly Stillman to win the Girls' 18 Division. Tracy didn't lose a single set during the entire competition in the two divisions.

Tracy moved into the big time in 1977 by entering the $20,000 Avon Futures tourney in Portland, Oregon. As a junior amateur she would be competing against seasoned pros.

Avon had put together a nationwide, 10-tournament schedule with

Tracy ducks a ball during doubles match at Virginia Slims tournament in Los Angeles.

$205,000 in prize money. None of that money could go to Tracy because of her amateur standing. But that wasn't as important as this: If Tracy made it to the semi-finals, she could qualify for the Virginia Slims tour coming up. There, she'd be competing with the world's best.

World Tennis Magazine summed it up nicely. "That's what 14-year-old Tracy Austin and another cute blonde California teenager, Stacy Margolin (17), did during the circuit's very first stop in Portland. These sunshine kids, playing hooky from school, ran through the women pros like a couple of double-bladed scythes through long grass." *Both* made it to the finals.

By February, Tracy was playing her third Virginia Slims pro women's tennis tournament. It was at the L.A. Sports Arena. She had won her way there in qualifying tourneys in Houston and Minneapolis, shortly before.

The big event was her match with Rosie Casals, fifth seeded player. Rosie was ranked fourth in the world the year before. But first, she took on Lindsey Beaven. It was a routine win which she took 6-3, 6-4. Later, in a doubles match with Kate Latham, she lost to Brigitte Cuypers and Marise Kruger. Latham and Tracy hadn't practiced together before the match, which may explain the defeat.

Tracy showed her stuff in the Casals match, though she lost to Rosie 6-4, 6-4. She played better than she did in the Beaven match, making Rosie fight for every point. "I had to struggle," Rosie said. "I had to work hard .... I had to run up, back, and sideways...." Several games went to deuce (tie) and at times Tracy turned what seemed sure

These are some of Tracy's friends from the Southern California section. They pose here at Shreveport, La., during the Nationals for girls 14-and-under in 1976.

The U.S.L.T.A. GIRLS' 12 YR. NATIONAL CHAMPIONSHIP.. JULY 22-27-1974 Chatham Tennis Club, Savannah, Ga.

Can you recognize Tracy in this
Girls National Champions

points for Rosie into her own.

During the press conference later, Rosie kidded Tracy. "It's past your bed-time," she said. Turning to Mrs. Austin, she asked, "Want to take her home?" Then she added, "Wait till she [Tracy] gets twenty to thirty pounds heavier!"

Julie Heldman, once third ranked among U.S. women players, said of Tra-cy, "She is amazing. She hits the ball harder than most women much older and much stronger. She is very fast on the court and is not afraid to take the net where she is an excellent volleyer." People began comparing her to Chris Evert. Like Evert, Tracy is a right-hand-er who hits a two-fisted backhand.

Two months before Wimbledon, Tracy was at Hilton Head Island, S.C. The *Family Circle Magazine* Cup was her fifth tournament on the professional circuit. It was another testing ground to

Tracy laughs with Julie Heldman, once the third-ranked among U.S. women tennis players.

prove if she was ready for Wimbledon. In this meet, Tracy reached the quarter finals. She beat Dianne Fromholtz, 7-5, 6-4. It marked her first victory over a player ranked in the world's top 10 (Dianne ranked 8).

In the next weeks there would be other tournaments, Tracy would win those too. But it was her performance on the professional circuit that counted. Wimbledon and Forest Hills were suddenly within reach.

Tracy, 14, had dreamed of them since she was seven. Now, she was ready and eager to take them on.

CHAPTER FOUR

STRAWBERRIES
AND CREAM
AND *WIMBLEDON!*

Tracy arrived in London on a cold, rainy June morning, wide-eyed, happy, curious, excited, and filled with a sense of awe. She was to play at Wimbledon, the youngest player ever to be invited in its hundred year history. 128 tournament wins had boosted her to 23rd place in the world among women tennis players. She had earned the right.

It was a special honor. 1977 marked the 91st tournament in the Lawn Tennis

Championships on Grass (two world wars interrupted play). But Britain was celebrating the Centennial. There would be special events—teas, dinner dances, parties, a fancy Ball. Friday, July 1, Queen Elizabeth II would visit Wimbledon and present trophies on Centre Court to the women champions.

For Tracy, the weeks in England were Christmas and Disneyland, rolled into one. Followed by photographers and newspeople, she received the attention usually reserved for big celebrities. Her picture made the front pages of London's three most important newspapers. She became known as the Alice in Wonderland, the Super Kid, and Little Miss Marvel to thousands of Britains.

She'd sit with her mother in the lobby of the Gloucester Hotel and gape at the famous faces going by. Billie Jean King stopped and said she should keep a diary for the future. Arthur Ashe introduced himself. "I looked down and this glorious little face with that mouth full of railroad tracks was staring up. She's so *tiny!*"

Ilie Nastase passed by, and Tracy tugged at her mother's sleeve. "Look! Look! It's *him!* Oh Mom, don't look!" she squealed.

Wimbledon is the Rolls Royce of all tennis championships. It is the last great grass-court tournament. Fifty weeks of each year the 15 courts are seeded and pampered especially for the two week spectacular.

Tracy had competed on grass only twice before. The first time was in the national 18-and-under tourney. In that she reached the final round of 16. Then, in early June, she played a grass tournament in Scotland, as a kind of "warm up."

She had been told that the velvet green texture of Wimbledon's courts produced a fast, low skidding surface. Often the ball doesn't even bounce. She knew there had been many spectacular volleys in previous tournaments. But these had developed out of player desperation. If you didn't hit the ball before it landed, it might die. The players who performed best at Wimbledon were the big serve-and-volley types. Serves were Tracy's weakness.

Picture the first day. Those scheduled to play are spending quiet hours psyching themselves up for the game, or taking lunch. But activity at the All England Lawn Tennis and Croquet Club is reaching a peak.

It takes 1,500 people to make Wimbledon tick. Court coverers and cleaners, secretaries, volunteers from the fire brigade, uniformed men who man the gates. There are scoreboard operators, ticket sellers and takers, umpires, ball boys, linespeople, and many, many more.

Only one out of every three who apply for tickets are lucky enough to buy entrance before the games. So, each night hundreds camp outdoors, hoping to be first next day to snag one of 300 extra tickets to Centre Court.

Buses begin arriving before noon. They carry schoolchildren in blazers and plaids, couples with lunch baskets, old people with field glasses. Hear the program sellers, and food vendors calling their wares. Smell the hot pork pies and sandwiches. Taste the mouth-watering big, sweet strawberries, covered with cream.

Relaxing before Wimbledon.

At 1:50 p.m. on June 20th, the crowd of 14,000 around Centre Court stood up. Their applause swelled. The Band of the Welsh Guards, in scarlet uniforms, brass instruments gleaming, marched out to the green. They played "March of the Kings" from the opera *Aida*. Then, 41 of the 52 living singles champions of Wimbledon strode out. The guests of honor included the only men to win the Grand Slam of tennis. They marched along a crimson carpet, past a table draped in pea green on which silver medals glistened. Dan Maskell, voice of tennis on British TV, called their names and championship years. The Duke of Kent presented each with a specially struck commemorative medal.

The first players waited nervously in changing rooms in the clubhouse. At Wimbledon, women players change for matches in a three-level status setup. The better you are, the higher up you remove your clothes. Some feel that a woman playing her first Wimbledon doesn't just want to win the tournament. Her first goal is to do well enough to work her way out of the crowded basement to the middle level. And finally, all the way up to the top, to the Members' Changing Room. There, she'll find a color TV, a massage room, and be closest to Centre Court.

Each changing room has a different color towel. Players bring towels out to the courts. So, everyone knows when a player walks out what level of achievement he or she is at ... just by the color of his or her towel!

In *World Tennis* Magazine, Billie Jean King described how it felt to wait for your call to Centre Court.

"You sit there on hard bench seats

looking at your opponent. It is tough to make small talk when you are about to go out and battle. Sometimes we are given flowers. You can concentrate on the petals and the fragrance and act like you are a million miles from Centre Court."

Finally, Peter, the escort to Centre Court, says, "You are on." He checks the blue light which signals when royalty is watching. If it's on, you will curtsy to the Royal Box. Then, he escorts you from the waiting room to Centre Court.

Tracy played her first game on the third day of the tournament. She came to the court wearing a white tennis dress that looked like a French maid's apron. There was a big bow in back. A big pocket in front was used to hold her second ball, when serving. She wore a gold necklace and two tiny bracelets which she shook back often. Her hair was tied back by two pink bands.

.

51

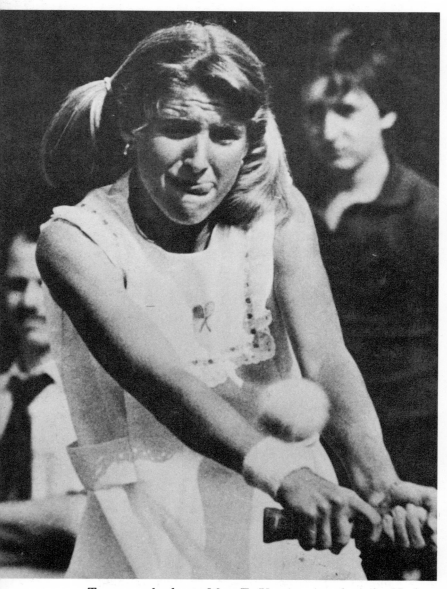
*Tracy as she beats Mrs. E. Vessies-Appel of the Nether-
lands at Wimbledon.*

At 9, Tracy took the 12-and-under title in the Los Angeles Junior Tennis tourney. She also won the 10-and-under division.

Showing very little emotion, she took on Elly Vessies-Appel of the Netherlands. She volleyed from the baseline like a Chris Evert. She covered the court like a Billie Jean King.

Tracy won the first point. The first game. The first set, and the first match of her Wimbledon career, 6-3, 6-3. It wasn't until the last point that she showed her feelings. She gave a little "whoop." Then she pranced to the net to shake hands with her opponent. Grinning at the crowds and newspeople, she said, "I played it just like any other match."

Before going to England with Tracy, Bob Lansdorp, her coach spoke to reporters. "I think Tracy is more advanced in most categories except the serve," he said. "She has good ground strokes. A good volley. And good attack. She's really quite an all-round player.

Tracy plays the whole court. Other youngsters are mostly baseline players at that age. Playing the whole court will help her on grass."

Lansdorp also said Tracy could do well depending on "who she draws." If she didn't draw the top eight, he said he would be happy. "But she has to be realistic. If she has a good showing, that's all we can expect."

Tracy drew for her next match not only from the top eight. But the top seeded player—Cris Evert! Could she beat Chris? "I don't think this year," Tracy said.

In 1972, Chris at 16 became the youngest semi-finalist ever to play at Forest Hills. She was the Wimbledon champ in 1974 and 1976. She has been No. 1 in the world on the women's circuit for four years.

Their match was played on Centre

Court at 5:15 in the afternoon. It was one of the week's highlights. The crowd pulled for Tracy. They rose to their feet and cheered wildly whenever she played long rallies from the baseline with Chris. Bands of children who were unable to get inside the playing grounds watched the results on the electric scoreboard from outside. "Tracy! Tracy! Tracy!" they screamed over and over. They were Tracy's private fan club.

Chris, 22, was nervous at first, losing the opening game. In the locker room she'd told Billie Jean King how she felt. "Don't worry Chris," Billie Jean had said. "It's just the way I felt when I first went out against you."

The first game of the match and the 11th went to Tracy. But Chris was in control during most of the forty-nine minutes, defeating Tracy 6-1, 6-1. But there's more to the story. Chris won only 62% of

Chris Evert stands with Tracy after beating her at Wimble-don, 6-1, 6-1.

the points, 61 to 38. Eight of the 14 games went to deuce. Among the other six were Tracy's two successful service games which she won at 30 and 15. Tracy also had seven break points in four separate games (this is when a player needs only one more point to win a game). Most of these she gave away through errors on service returns. Chris said later, "Tracy's got more variety than I had at 14. Maybe her volleys are better than mine already."

England's Ted Tinling has seen some 50 Wimbledons. He said, "I think she is a better player than Chrissy was when she came up. She has more power and she is a better volleyer."

After the match Chris put an arm around Tracy. The two of them then faced the Royal Box. They curtsied just as they had done before start of play.

With Wimbledon over, Tracy returned to the United States. Happy memories crowded her head as she flew home. Memories of curtsying to royalty. Of screaming fans. Of plump, red strawberries in thick, sweet cream.

But she would have to put these thoughts aside to look at later. The tournament season wasn't over. Still to come was another big challenge—the U.S. Open at Forest Hills.

Jeanne Austin watches Tracy play at Forest Hills.

CHAPTER FIVE

FOREST HILLS - "I DID IT MOM!"

Just a few days before starting high school, Tracy was in New York. She was playing in the last U.S. Open to be held at Forest Hills. Soon a larger site will be built at the 1964 World's Fair grounds nearby in Flushing.

The 1977 U.S. Open featured many of the world's best women players. But the crowds adopted two favorites: Wendy Turnbull—who earned the nickname

"Rabbit" for her speed—and Tracy, "The Kid."

Again, Tracy was being compared to Chris Evert. Both had won the U.S. National juniors before going on to Forest Hills. Chris did it at the age of 16 and reached the semi-finals. How far would Tracy go at Forest Hills?

In her first round, Tracy played against Heidi Eisterlehner. Heidi, a German, has a wicked top-spin backhand. But she was no match for Tracy. The score was 3-6, 6-3, 6-1 for Tracy.

In her second match, Tracy beat Donna Ganz. Then, she was pitted against Britain's Sue Barker.

Barker has a long list of credits: winner of the French Open, Wimbledon semi-finalist, runnerup to Chris Evert in three tough sets in the Virginia Slims final. She earns in the six-figure bracket, and ranks fourth among women tennis players in the world.

Everything Tracy did went right, from the beginning. She seemed to be out-thinking Sue all the way. Sue didn't seem able to change her game. She might have slowed the pace, or come to the net. She might have drawn Tracy in and lobbed over her. Tracy appeared totally unafraid. She kept hitting to Sue's forehand, even though most players fear it because it's so hard.

The first set went to Tracy 6-1. She was ahead 3-0 by the middle of the second set after winning eight straight games. Then, Sue seemed to bounce back some. But Tracy's ground strokes and her ability to pin Sue to the baseline were too much. The set ended with Sue Barker hitting a backhand volley beyond the baseline. Tracy let out a little shriek. She popped a ball straight up and sprinted to the net. There, she shook hands with Sue. Tracy took the fifty-nine minute match 6-1, 6-4. The stadium went wild.

Tracy called it the biggest win of her life. On the way to the interview tent she stopped to hug her parents and coach. "I did it mom!" she cried joyfully.

Next, Tracy took on Romania's Virginia Ruzici. If she could get by her, and then beat Betty Stove, she'd be a Forest Hills semi-finalist at 14. She'd probably play Chris again in the finals.

The odds of Tracy's beating Ruzici were good. Ruzici, 22, was a very solid player on clay courts. If they played on an outside court, Tracy had a 55% chance of winning. If inside the stadium, the odds improved to 75%. They played inside.

Ruzici's big forehands and smashes caused Tracy more trouble than Bark-

Tracy in action against Rosemary Casals.

er's. Their fourth round match was before a stadium of over 12,000 people. It lasted one hour and forty minutes, forty-one minutes longer than with Barker. When it was over, Ruzici was tired and frustrated. She had hit one bullet ground stroke after another and the ball came back deeper nearly every time. She made 25 more errors than Tracy (61 to 36) which made the difference.

Tracy was tired, too, but very happy. She had beat Ruzici 6-3, 7-5 and had reached the quarter-finals of her first U.S. Open. If she beat her next opponent, she would equal Chris's record at an earlier age.

Tracy had four solid wins behind her (Eisterlehner, Ganz, Barker and Ruzici). Now, she had to face 32-year-old Betty Stove of The Netherlands. Betty was a finalist against Virginia Wade at Wimbledon. At 6'1" and 160 pounds, she overshadowed Tracy by one foot and 67 pounds. It was a match between David and Goliath.

"That was one of the best matches I ever played," Stove said later, after her win. Stove hit dozens of 90 m.p.h. zingers in the fifty-six minute 6-2, 6-2 victory. She could have beaten a lot of grown-up professionals.

Stove was the better player, but the fans were for Tracy. They applauded every time Betty made a mistake. It didn't matter. It was the giant's day.

Jeff, Tracy's older brother said, "Betty just out-bigged her." From the start she had "The Kid" squeaking in frustration as she tried to stretch beyond her short reach. Betty used very clever tactics. She hit behind Tracy at the baseline. Or brought her up to the net, then hit offensive lobs over her outstretched racket.

"There was nothing I could do," Tracy said afterward. "I could barely get her serve back. I never saw anyone serve so hard. She just overpowered me. We didn't have any rallies. She just put the ball away. I didn't run much at all. She just hit winners."

Tracy's loss to Stove was nothing to be ashamed of. Betty Stove had played the best tennis of her life. Her record was admirable. Tracy will come up against Stove again. Then, she will be taller and heavier, and Betty will be older. The match between the two will be more equal.

For now though, it was enough to leave Forest Hills as a quarter-finalist. Tracy had trounced four professionals, including one of the world's top women players. Herds of kids trailed after her. Newspaper reporters and photographers hung on her words. Fans num-

Taking a break between games.

bered in the thousands. She was the darling of the tennis world.

Just before leaving Forest Hills, Tracy received a phone call. She rushed from the locker room to take it. A voice said, "Tracy, this is Jimmy Carter." Tracy gulped. A call from the President!! "I just watched you on television, and you were wonderful," he said. "If you ever find yourself in Washington, please come by and see me." Tracy was so nervous, all she could say was, "Yeah. Yeah. Thank you. Thank you."

For a pig-tailed little kid of 14 just about to start ninth grade, 1977 had been one great summer. But the years ahead look even brighter. At Wimbledon, Tracy was billed as the Future Queen of Tennis when she played Chris Evert. If she lives up to her promise, it won't be long before the word "Future" is changed to "Now."

A moment to fix her hair.

Tracy gives some tips at a free tennis workshop at the L.A. Tennis Club.

CHAPTER SIX

WHAT TRACY'S COACHES SAY

Few junior players have what it takes to be a Tracy. Most would be happy to be among the best in their sectional. Or, joy of joys, to be selected for the Nationals. Here is what Tracy's coaches have to say about being a winner:

Vic Braden, Tracy's first teacher, coached the rest of the Austin family for almost 10 years. Now directing the Vic Braden Tennis College in southern California, he is author of the very popular *Tennis for the Future* with Bill Bruns.

Braden says Tracy was engineered to be a pro from the day she was born. "She was an intense competitor from the first. While other little girls played with dolls, she preferred tennis balls. Tracy *should* be winning," he says. "She has a mother who cares and calculates. From day one she's had coaching not only from me and Lansdorp, but from her sister and brothers. She had the advantage of playing college-age kids in drills when she was only seven."

Asked what helpful suggestions he could give other young players, Braden listed five.

1. Appreciate tennis as a sport. Tennis is beautiful to play, the greatest sport of all. Enjoy tennis for itself. Don't worry about winning championships.

Tracy playing Sue Barker at Forest Hills, N.Y. Tracy won, 6-1, 6-4.

2. Tennis should help build character. Fairness, court etiquette, good sportsmanship are the qualities to develop. With those qualities, you'll always be worth knowing.

3. Know what's going on. Concentrate. Become aware of what's happening physically and emotionally on the court. Understand what happens to a ball when it hits the strings at any angle. Know what angle to position your racket for the best results.

4. Learn to practice so you get the best use of your time.

5. Study your opponents. Play to their weaknesses. Compensate for their strengths.

Braden was asked if it mattered what balls or rackets were used. He favors no particular balls. He said they were all about the same in play-ability and wear. As to whether to use a wood

Tracy has been compared with tennis greats such as Helen Wills, upper right; Maureen "Little Mo" Connolly, upper left; and Chris Evert, lower left.

or metal frame racket, he said that didn't matter, either. "Both rackets are engineered beyond the player's limits. However," he said, "a junior racket should be strung to about 50 pounds. Adult rackets should be strung to 55-60 pounds."

Robert Lansdorp has been Tracy's coach for eight years. Tracy now takes three hour-long lessons from him each week. Part of the time she practices at the Jack Kramer Club near home. Part of the time she practices at the West End Tennis Club which Lansdorp co-directs. She is on the courts from three to four hours a day, every day.

Lansdorp has great affection for Tracy, but he drives her hard. In an interview with Ted Green of the *Los Angeles Times*, he said, "Sometimes I will irritate her just to get her mad. If she's just going through the motions I yell at

Wherever Tracy plays, photographers, reporters and fans follow her.

Tracy chats with friends on her first day at Rolling Hills High School.

her. 'Who do you think you are? What is this?' She'll say, 'I'm tired.' And I'll say, 'I've been here eight hours already. I'm tired too!'

"Then the war is on. I tell her I'm gonna beat the daylights out of her. I make her run wide to the backhand and forehand, corner to corner, ten times. Do that drill often enough, it's hyper-ventilation time. After that, I might bunch four balls in a corner as a target and tell her she has ten shots to hit the target. Tracy needs a challenge. It's the only way to keep her interested. The first time, maybe she goes zero for ten. Then I say, 'If you don't want to run ten along the baseline, you better concen-trate and hit those darn balls.'

"All of a sudden you see the feisti-ness in her. She'll run her guts out once we start playing. She'll go for every point and attack every ball. Afterwards,

Tracy, with her brother John, at Rolling Hills High School.

Beating Virginia Ruzici at Forest Hills.

we hug each other. I don't like having to be mean, but sometimes it's a must."

Tracy has cried at Lansdorp's discipline. But she also realizes he is only trying to help her.

When Lansdorp was asked to list the most important qualities needed to be a winner, he gave these:

1. Athletic ability. Players need to have good eye-hand coordination, and timing. They need to know how to move well. Some of these characteristics can be taught. But the natural athlete is born with them.

2. The coach is possibly as important as athletic ability. He or she can correct weaknesses, strengthen assets, make the student use his abilities to the utmost. The coach can push the abilities beyond the limit.

3. The desire to suceed. Without

Playing Sue Barker, at the U.S. Open Tennis match at Forest Hills.

that, no player can reach the top, no matter how natural her athletic ability, or how good her coach.

4. Practicing regularly and using practice time well is very important. Just rallying isn't enough. Each minute on the court must be used to improve the game. Intense concentration is a must.

5. Parent cooperation helps. Parents must be behind the player, willing to give time, money and encouragement.

Both coaches stress pretty much the same things. But Braden adds one more point about the future. "Coaching is improving so rapidly that the next generation of juniors is sure to be better than the last. Then Tracy, who may well be better than Chris, will find there's another Tracy coming up who may be better than she."

Tracy takes a moment to relax with the family pet.